POWERING UP
A CAREER IN
NANOTECHNOLOGY

KRISTI LEW

ROSEN
PUBLISHING®
New York

Published in 2016 by The Rosen Publishing Group, Inc.
29 East 21st Street, New York, NY 10010

Copyright © 2016 by The Rosen Publishing Group, Inc.

First Edition

Library of Congress Cataloging-in-Publication Data

Lew, Kristi, author.
Powering up a career in nanotechnology/Kristi Lew.—First edition.
    pages cm.—(Preparing for tomorrow's careers)
ISBN 978-1-4994-6087-2 (library bound)
1. Nanotechnology—Vocational guidance—Juvenile literature.
2. Nanotechnology—Juvenile literature. [1. Vocational guidance.]
I. Title.
T174.7.L49 2016
620.5023—dc23
                                                    2014042464

Manufactured in the United States of America

CONTENTS

INTRODUCTION

I f you could build something atom by atom, molecule by molecule, what would it be? Would you build a tiny disease-detecting robot that could maneuver through the human bloodstream and destroy cancerous cells on sight? Or would you design a new molecule that could neutralize radioactive waste, solving the storage and potential exposure problems that plague today's nuclear industry? Or maybe you would turn your eye toward building lighter, stronger body armor that could better protect police and military forces during conflict. These ideas may sound like science fiction, but the men and women employed in the cutting-edge field of nanotechnology are diligently working toward making all of them scientific fact.

Nanotechnology is the study and application of extremely small things. Most nanotechnology careers involve the intersection of science and engineering. In the narrowest of definitions, science is the investigation of the natural world

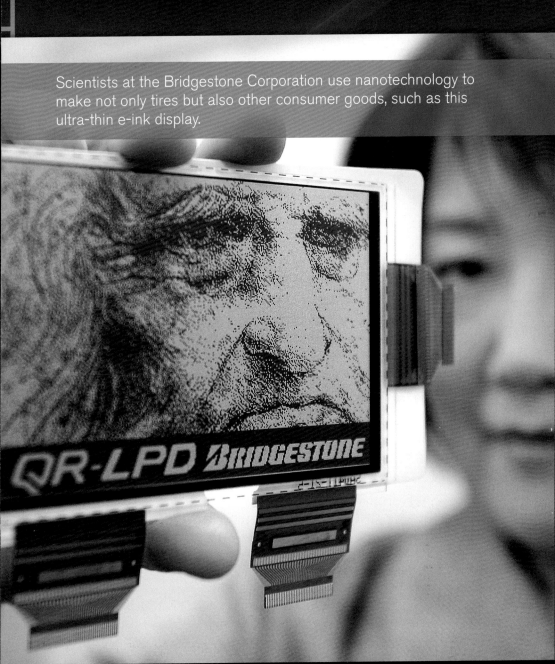

Scientists at the Bridgestone Corporation use nanotechnology to make not only tires but also other consumer goods, such as this ultra-thin e-ink display.

and engineering is the design and development of new products and technologies. In reality, the areas of science and engineering overlap and influence one another. For example, scientists rely on the technologies designed by engineers—such as microscopes, detectors, and other equipment—to do their research. Engineers rely on the scientific knowledge discovered by researchers to inform their designs. The needs of society and the problems society faces also influence the questions that scientists ask and subsequently research, as well as the new technologies engineers design and develop.

For the first time in history, scientists and engineers have developed the tools that allow them not only to see atoms but also to manipulate and move them into new arrangements like never before, creating new materials and opening up tremendous possibilities for the future. Scientists predict that nanotechnology will become increasingly more important over the coming decades and will eventually touch every area of human life. Because the possibilities are so vast, experts expect nanoscale science and technology to create numerous new and exciting careers at many different levels—from skilled technicians to university researchers with doctorate degrees.

These predictions are based on the multitude of scientists and engineers currently working in this rewarding field. According to an article in the *Journal of Nanoparticle Research*, products enabled with nanotechnology brought in about $40 billion in 2000. Nine years later, that amount had increased to almost $250 billion. The increase in market value was also accompanied by an increase in jobs—from about 60,000 nanotechnology workers in 2000 to nearly 400,000 by 2009. Experts predict the market value of nanotechnology products will reach $1 trillion by 2020. As a result, the National Science Foundation anticipates that the nanotechnology sector will employ nearly one million U.S. workers by 2015 and the field will continue to grow from there.

As these statistics show, opportunities in nanotechnology are expanding rapidly. Scientists imagine using nanoscale science to better understand and enhance the fields of medicine, imaging, computing, printing, chemical manufacturing, and material science. To give some examples, a profession in nanoscale science may involve the development of increasingly small medical devices, the design of improved automobile or aeronautical manufacturing processes, the creation of new cosmetics or fabrics, or the production of better, faster, and smaller computers. These fields, and many more, are going to require a new generation of skilled workers. With education and training, you could be one of these individuals.

CHAPTER ONE

IT'S A SMALL WORLD AFTER ALL

What much of the general public does not realize is that nanotech (short for nanotechnology) is not some far-off technology. Many people are already using it, whether they know it or not. In recent years, scientists have discovered ways to apply nanotechnology to the fields of medicine, robotics, textiles, cosmetics, computers, and the environment. In addition, advances in nanotechnology are announced nearly every day. In the future, scientists expect nanotech to progress even more, potentially reshaping many of the world's current industries.

The term *nanotechnology* was popularized by an American engineer named K. Eric Drexler in the 1980s. Since then, the term has come to have two meanings. The media often apply the term *nanotechnology* to anything that possesses parts or components that are less than 100 nanometers in size. Most scientists call this nanoscale technology. The original meaning of the term *nanotechnology*, and the way it is most commonly used in scientific circles, refers to the design and building of molecular machines and structures in which every atom and every bond between those atoms is specified. In other words, designing and building a product from the ground up—atom by atom.

8

Nanotechnology pioneer K. Eric Drexler displays a large-scale model of a robot he designed. In the background, a computer model renders the individual atoms of the robot in orange and gray.

OLD CONCEPT, NEW UNDERSTANDING

Although modern nanoscale technology is a relatively new field, nanoparticles are not new in science or in nature. Nanoparticles occur naturally all around people—the smoke from a fire, volcanic ash, and sea spray are all nanoscale materials. At the nanoscale, quantum effects rule the properties and behaviors of particles. When materials are made in the 1- to 100-nanometer range, the range where particles can only be "seen" with powerful, specialty electron microscopes, the material's properties can be strikingly different from those at larger scales. Qualities such as melting point, fluorescence, electrical conductivity, magnetic behavior, and chemical reactivity change as the size of the particles change.

Humans have been using the unique properties of some nanoparticles for hundreds of years. For example, artists who designed medieval stained glass windows used the unique optical properties of gold and silver nanoparticles to create a rainbow of colors. Gold particles, which appear yellow to the human eye on the macroscopic scale, are red or purple on the nanoscale. The reason for the difference in color is related to the way electrons in a gold nanoparticle move compared to those on a larger scale. Because of this distinction in movement, the electrons interact with light differently and reflect varying wavelengths of light, which translates into different colors. These ancient artisans did not know that they were working with nanoparticles; they simply liked the effect.

Relatively recent advances in microscopy and other scientific areas have allowed scientists to better understand and take advantage of the properties of nanoscale materials. Today, scientists are experimenting with distinct ways to manipulate matter at the atomic level. Although many people think of computers when nanotechnology is mentioned, this field of study is not limited just to making

HOW SMALL IS SMALL?

The prefix *nano-* comes from a Greek word meaning "dwarf." Scientists who work in nanotechnology deal with structures that are much too tiny to be seen with the human eye. These structures are measured in nano-meters (nm), or one-billionth of a meter (m). What does one-billionth of a meter look like? The following are some comparisons:

- One nanometer is 100,000 times smaller than the width of a human hair.
- Seven oxygen atoms or three to four water molecules lined up side by side would be about 1 nm across.
- A red blood cell is approximately 7,000 nm wide.
- A sheet of paper is about 100,000 nm thick.
- The period at the end of this sentence is about 300,000 nm across.
- One foot measures more than 304 million nm.
- A strand of human DNA is about 2.5 nm in diameter, which is approximately 1,000 times smaller than the length of a single bacterium.

In other words, it's really, really small.

smaller and smaller computer components. It also means understanding and utilizing the unique physical, chemical, mechanical, and optical properties of matter that naturally occur on this scale. These properties have some exciting practical applications.

THE FUTURE IS NOW

This richly colored stained glass window from around 1300 depicts a barrel seller. Medieval artisans took advantage of the unique optical properties of gold and silver nanoparticles to create the brilliant reds and yellows used in stained glass.

Similar to the stained glass artisans of the Middle Ages, people today are making use of nanoparticles— this time, on purpose. It turns out that tiny particles of silver not only make beautiful colored glass; they are also deadly to bacteria. Textile chemists have made use of this fact and developed a way to impregnate fabric and other materials with silver nanoparticles. Using these nano-enabled materials, the textile industry has been able to make self-sanitizing toothbrushes, bacteria-resistant stuffed animals, and less stinky socks.

Socks saturated with silver nanoparticles are not the only wearable product made possible by nanotechnology. The makers of colored contact lenses have been using nanosized particles of pigment to make brown eyes blue since the mid-2000s. Going one step further, engineers have recently developed contact lenses that contain optical elements smaller than the human pupil. Tiny projectors, possibly mounted on a pair of eyeglasses, activate the optical elements in the contact lenses but the normal field of vision remains unimpaired. The end result sounds like something straight out of a science fiction novel. When the projectors are switched on, images— such as data, games, movies, simulated environments, and other applications—are seamlessly superimposed over what the eye normally sees. These contact lenses could eventually make virtual reality an actual reality, without having to rely on bulky head-mounted monitors.

Another current application of nanotechnology is in the field of composite materials. Numerous industries are using these materials and they are looking for scientists who can develop more. A composite is a material that is made by combining two or more separate components with differing physical and chemical properties. By combining components, the resulting material has properties that the separate components do not. Typically, composites are produced to improve the strength of a material, to make it lighter, or to make it less expensive to manufacture or buy. Some automobile manufacturers are using plastic nanocomposites to make lightweight and scratch- and dent-resistant bumpers. Sporting goods

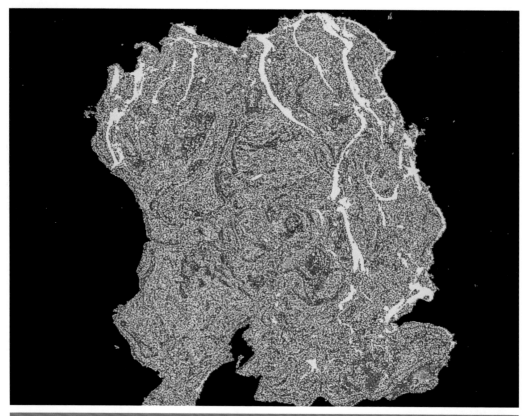

A nanocomposite developed by the Pacific Northwest National Laboratories is shown under a scanning electron microscope. This porous nanomaterial could one day turn contaminated waterways into sources of purified drinking water.

manufacturers use nanocomposites to make stronger, lighter golf clubs, tennis rackets, and high-tech bicycles. Researchers at the Pacific Northwest National Laboratories have developed a nanocomposite that selectively attaches to toxic metals in water. This spongelike composite sops up heavy-metal contaminants, such as mercury and lead.

The industries mentioned here are just a few of the fields in which nanotechnology is currently being used.

WHOSE IDEA WAS THIS?

The idea of exploring the infinitesimal world of nanotechnology got a big boost on December 29, 1959. On that date, Richard Feynman (1918–1988), an American physicist, gave a speech titled "There's Plenty of Room at the Bottom" to a group of scientists at an American Physical Society meeting. During the speech, held at the California Institute of Technology (Caltech) in Pasadena, Feynman issued two challenges. The first challenge was to make a working electric motor that would fit inside a cube that was only one sixty-fourth of an inch (0.41 millimeter) on each side. He offered a $1,000 reward to the first person to do so. To Feynman's surprise, this challenge was met just a few months later by an American electrical engineer named William McLellan. McLellan successfully made a working motor just 0.016 inch (0.41 millimeter) long and claimed his $1,000 prize.

Feynman's second challenge took quite a bit longer for scientists to figure out. His second challenge was to shrink the print on the page of a book so that it was 25,000 times smaller than the standard print size. At this size, the text of an entire set of the Encyclopædia

(continued on the next page)

(continued from the previous page)

Britannica, which was comprised of twenty-four volumes in 1959, would fit on the head of a pin. Again, Feynman offered a $1,000 reward to the first person that rose to the challenge. That person was Thomas Newman, a graduate student in electrical engineering at Stanford University. Using a beam of electrons, Newman successfully reduced the first page of Charles Dickens's novel *A Tale of Two Cities* to the required size and etched it onto the head of a pin. Newman claimed his prize in 1985, just three years before Richard Feynman died of cancer.

Research is even more widespread. No matter what your interest—whether it is computers, medicine, environmentalism, food science, textile chemistry, or some other field—it is likely that someone in that industry is exploring how nanotechnology could be used in it. The areas in which nanotechnology is being explored and the expertise of the people who work within these areas are constantly evolving. However, the men and women who work in nanotechnology careers do tend to have one thing in common—an interest and aptitude for mathematics and science.

CHAPTER TWO

THINK BIG (AND SMALL)

Nanotechnology is very much an interdisciplinary field, meaning that it can be applied across many areas of science, including physics, chemistry, biology, material science, and engineering. In the future, it is likely that the scope of nanotechnology will grow even broader. In short, nanotechnology today could be described as a science-intensive field of engineering. It is where science and engineering intersect and overlap. Unlike current engineering fields in which conventional materials are used to construct products that solve societal problems, engineers working in the field of nanotechnology are much more likely to have to find a way, through experimentation, to make the object that they have conceived of—often from materials or by using techniques that do not yet exist. More and more the nanotechnology field will need people with a background that allows them to understand the science underlying the technology as well as the engineering problem-solving skills necessary to utilize that knowledge.

POWERFUL PREPARATION

Because nanoscale science and nanotechnology focus on the raw materials of matter—atoms and

A solid foundation in math, science, and engineering can lead to a rewarding career in the cutting-edge field of nanotechnology.

molecules—these fields tie together all of the sciences. If you're interested in launching a career in nanotechnology, you will need to understand the properties and interactions of matter. Nanoscale science is a little unique in that scientists from diverse fields of study collaborate to explore the nanoscale world from many different perspectives. In that way, there are many divergent avenues that will allow entry into the world of nanotechnology. An understanding of basic physics—including classical mechanics as well as electromagnetism—is very useful knowledge in this field. A foundation in chemistry, an understanding of chemical synthesis, knowledge of the structure and function of biomolecules, and how intermolecular forces work would also serve you well. Thermodynamics and quantum mechanics are also fields you might like to explore. Because mathematics is the language of science, a good grasp of the subject can go a long way. Engineering and the understanding of how engineers solve problems are also necessary. Studying science or engineering in school and paying attention to the developments in the field will provide a solid foundation for a wide variety of jobs in the future.

Successful candidates for a nanotechnology career tend to have an excellent understanding of science and mathematics. They are also creative problem-solvers, detail-oriented, and comfortable using a variety of computer hardware and software programs, such as engineering computer-aided design (CAD) software.

Nanotechnology fields need people with a wide variety of educational levels, including technical (high school plus extra training), associate's degrees (two years of college), bachelor's degrees (four years of college), master's degrees (about six years of college), and doctorate degrees (about nine years of college). Nanotechnology engineering technicians usually have technical training or an associate's degree in a scientific field. Technicians often work under the supervision of engineering staff members or senior nanoscale scientists. Nanotechnology technicians may assemble components, assist nanoscale scientists or engineers with experiments and documentation, or calibrate, maintain, and operate equipment necessary for those experiments. A four-year degree or beyond is generally needed to engage in nanoscale design work or research. Current salary ranges for each level of education and training can be found in the *Occupational Outlook Handbook* (http://www.bls.gov/ooh), published by the Bureau of Labor Statistics.

BEYOND THE BASICS

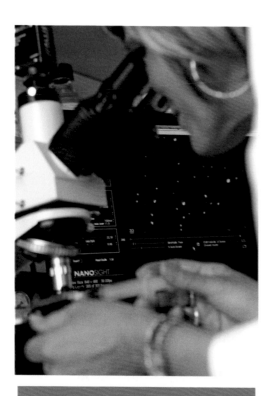

Obtaining technical training in a scientific discipline, such as biology, chemistry, or physics, can open many doors in the field of nanotechnology.

There are many universities, programs, and opportunities to study the numerous areas of science and engineering currently involved in nanoscale science. How do you choose which ones are right for you? First, decide what your objectives are. Where do your interests lie? Are you interested in making ever-smaller computers? Or are you interested in the possible medicinal applications of nanotechnology? One of the best ways to decide which areas of study would be most useful to you is to look through a college course of study in nanotechnology. Even if you do not plan to get an advanced degree, looking at the courses that are

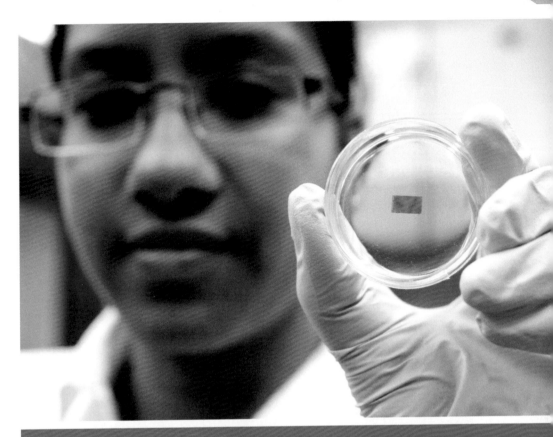

Completing an internship or a sponsored research project can help advanced high school and university students gain valuable hands-on research experience.

required may be helpful in narrowing the focus. Look at the prerequisites essential for each course in the science and engineering fields you are most interested in. These requirements can give you a good idea of which direction to choose.

Once you have decided on a direction, look for institutions or people who specialize in these areas. Universities should provide a degree program that fits

SIGNIFICANT EVENTS IN NANOTECHNOLOGY

Nanotechnology is a relatively new field. The following timeline includes some of the notable events that have made this area of study possible.

1955 A field ion microscope makes atoms visible for the first time.

1959 American physicist Richard Feynman issues his challenge; it is believed to be the real start of nanotechnology.

1960 A 0.4-millimeter electric motor is developed; it wins part of Feynman's challenge.

1974 Norio Taniguchi introduces the term *nanotechnology*.

1981 The scanning tunneling microscope (STM) is invented.

1985 The second of Feynman's challenges is won; buckminsterfullerenes (also called buckyballs or fullerenes) are discovered.

1986 The atomic force microscope (AFM) is developed; it allows individual atoms to be placed and moved.

1987 K. Eric Drexler publishes a book entitled *Engines of Creation: The Coming Era of Nanotechnology*; it popularizes the term *nanotechnology*.

1989 IBM researchers use the AFM to spell out the company's logo in individual atoms.

1991 Carbon nanotubes are discovered.

1997 The first company devoted to nanotechnology, Zyvex, is formed; researchers at Cornell make the first nano-guitar.

2000 Early nanoproducts, such as sunscreen and hair dyes, go on sale to the public.

2002 "Nano-care" clothing is developed.

2004 A study shows that fullerenes in the water can be harmful to fish.

2006 Researchers at Rice University in Houston, Texas, develop nanoparticles that remove arsenic from drinking water.

2010 Researchers create self-assembling nanodevices from DNA that can move and change shape on demand.

2012 The U.S. government recognizes the strategic importance of nanotechnology and sets aside $2 billion for research.

2013 The first fully functional nano-sized computer, made entirely of carbon nanotubes, is developed.

2014 Bioengineers inject nanorobots made of DNA into cockroaches. The nanobots successfully unfold and release medication when they encounter specified proteins.

your objectives and interests or have the flexibility to allow you to design your own course of study. Look at the textbooks required for the courses in the degree program you have selected. Skim through them and make notes on areas you could start exploring now. Do the same with science journals, such as *Science* and *Nature*. Study those ideas that interest you in depth, then circle back to the textbooks and journals to see what other concepts you can find to explore.

As you progress further with your education, these activities will help you in the courses you decide to take and the other activities you may find yourself engaged in. Look for research programs or internships for high school and undergraduate college students, such as the one conducted by the National Nanotechnology Infrastructure Network (NNIN). The ten-week-long NNIN program is designed to give students introductory research experience. Students may choose to conduct their research project at eleven different universities around the United States. The earlier you can become involved in hands-on research or applications in your chosen field, the better prepared you will be. If you have found companies in your area that are involved in nanoscale research, contact them and ask about research opportunities. The website Nano.gov can also help you find programs throughout the United States that award a certificate or an associate's degree in nanotechnology.

CLUBS FOR THE CLEVER

You have probably heard or read about the acronym STEM. STEM stands for science, technology, engineering, and mathematics. One way to get more information about STEM-related careers, including those of nanotechnology engineering technician or nanoscale scientist, and what it might be like to work in one of the careers is to join a STEM-related club. Some of the activities you might want to explore include those involving your school's computer, science, and math clubs. Competitions such as FIRST Robotics, MathCounts, and Science Olympiad, and

Students who participate in engineering challenges, such as the FIRST Robotics Competition, have thrilling events where they can learn skills in design and construction.

local, regional, and national science fairs are good places to look, too.

FIRST (For Inspiration and Recognition of Science and Technology) is an international youth organization that operates FIRST Robotics, the FIRST LEGO League, the Junior FIRST LEGO League, and the FIRST Tech Challenge competitions. The FIRST Tech Challenge (FTC) is a competition in which teams of up to ten high-school students design, build, and program robots. Awards, including millions of dollars in college scholarships, are given at the local, regional, national, and international levels. FTC students learn basic engineering principles to help them build their robots, including computer programming and computer-assisted design (CAD), skills that are invaluable to a future in nanotechnology. If there is not a team in the area where you live, the FIRST website can help you start one. The FIRST Robotics Competition is similar, but teams can be as large as twenty-five students. Often, these students work with and learn from professional engineers. Winning teams are also awarded scholarships to help pay for college. Programs like these can help you get involved in problem-solving and team-building activities that will serve you well in the years to come.

You can also enhance your résumé and make yourself more attractive to potential employers by teaching or doing volunteer work. You may choose to tutor middle school or elementary students in STEM-related subjects. Or maybe you can organize and found a FIRST Tech Challenge group or a Science Olympiad team. You may also consider volunteering your time to help your local Junior FIRST LEGO League, which teaches elementary school children how to design and build models using LEGO components. If you prefer to work with older students, there is also the FIRST LEGO League in which teams of middle school and early high-school students design and build LEGO robots to perform a series of preset missions.

Mentoring students in your local FIRST LEGO League can enhance your résumé and potentially make you more attractive to future employers.

CASH FOR COLLEGE

There are many funding options available for students who wish to pursue a STEM-related career. MathCounts, the FIRST Tech Challenge, and the FIRST Robotics Challenge are only a few programs that award scholarships for furthering a person's education. The Thermo Scientific Pierce Scholarship Program is another example. This

SOME HELPFUL TIPS

What are some of the important things to know about nanotechnology? Here are what some of the men and women currently working in the field have to say:

"I think math is something that frightens a lot of people off. But, not all areas of nanoscience require as much math as some people think. So, if math isn't your strong point, you're able to choose, perhaps, a more biological route into the field."
~ Dr. Amanda Petford-Long, the director of the Nanoscience and Technology Division, and Center for Nanoscale Materials at Argonne National Laboratory in an interview with *Helix* magazine

"Nano-wires may enable more precise and sensitive connections between human brains and machines controlled by those brains. There are concerns not only about the ethics and priority of this kind of research, but also about the equitable access to such technologies, should they come on line."
~ David Guston, director of the Arizona State University Center for Nanotechnology and Society in an interview with Arizona State University's *Research Matters*

"The long-range revolutionary potential of developments at the nanoscale will come from atomically precise manufacturing."
~ Dr. K. Eric Drexler in an interview with *Nanotechnology Now*

program awards scholarships to students majoring in biology, chemistry, biochemistry, or related scientific fields. Like many scholarships, this program requires that candidates have good grades. In this case, a freshman candidate must have a cumulative high school grade point average (GPA) of 3.0 or higher on a 4.0 scale.

You do not necessarily have to attend a four-year university to be awarded scholarship money. The Great Lakes Higher Education Corporation is a company that provides students with loans to help them pay for college. They also offer up to 750 scholarships that do not need to be paid back. These scholarships are awarded to students enrolled full-time at a public or private two-year college or university, a four-year college or university, or at a vocational-technical school and who have declared a STEM-related major. High school seniors who live in the United States, have a GPA of 2.75 or higher on a 4.0 scale, can demonstrate financial need, and are enrolled full-time at an accredited college, university, or vocational-technical school are eligible for these scholarship. Students may reapply for the scholarship each year that they meet the eligibility requirements.

These examples are just a few of the scholarships that are available for students who are thinking of studying a STEM-related field. Searching for STEM scholarships online will bring up many others along with their requirements and deadlines for application.

CHAPTER THREE

THE DIMINUTIVE DAY-TO-DAY

Perhaps you are interested in a nanotechnology career that will help make everyday life easier and safer for everyone? Textile chemists have used nanotechnology to create clothing resistant to wrinkles, stains, and water. Imagine what other problems might be solved with nano-enabled cloth. Men and women in the cosmetics field have used nanotechnology to develop sunscreen that goes on clear but still protects people from harmful ultraviolet rays. Forensic scientists in the Federal Bureau of Investigation (FBI), the Central Intelligence Agency (CIA), and local law enforcement are using nanotechnology to help solve crimes, and they are developing more procedures every day. Numerous scientists and engineers are working in the food science and agricultural industries, too. They are investigating ways to enhance the flavor of foods, enable food storage materials to alert people to potential problems, and to develop higher-yield, pest-resistant crops to feed everyone. How might you use your interests and skills in the future to advance one of these fields?

THE COMPETITIVE EDGE

The men and women who work in the textile industry use nanotechnology to develop yarn and cloth with unique properties. Textile chemists have found that coating fibers with specific nanoparticles, which are so small that they do not change the look or feel of the fabric, can impart desired characteristics such as stain and wrinkle resistance. Antibacterial socks, for example, contain silver nanoparticles, which are deadly to bacteria.

Companies that manufacture sporting goods apparel have developed fabrics that not only can wick away sweat and zap smelly bacteria but can also keep athletes safe. Working together, scientists and engineers have developed a cap made of silicon nanofibers that National Football League players can wear under their helmets. The nanofibers sense how many times and with what force the players have been hit in the head. The device contains a sensor that lights up, alerting a coach of the potential of a dangerous head injury. The same company that developed the cap has also developed a stick-on sensor that can tell athletes of all types—

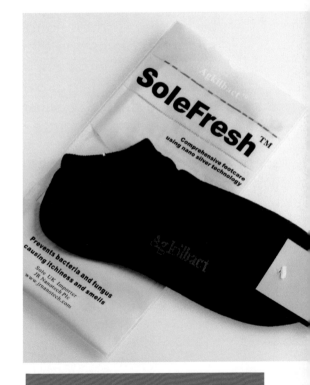

Impregnating cotton fibers with silver nanoparticles kills the bacteria responsible for stinky feet.

from professionals to weekend warriors—how hydrated they are. The device sends an alarm to a smart phone when it senses the wearer is getting dehydrated.

Experts predict that people will all be wearing more and more "smart" clothes, or wearable electronics, as time goes on. For electronics to be comfortable enough to wear, they will need to be small and lightweight. They will also necessitate a source of power. This requirement is where carbon nanotubes might be helpful. Carbon nanotubes are made from sheets of carbon atoms one atom thick that are rolled into a tube. These tubes are very good electrical conductors and could help provide the power needed. In the future, textile scientists and electrical engineers are likely to collaborate in the development of more and more applications of "smart" clothes.

But the use of carbon nanotubes in the textile industry is not relegated to the future. Currently, cloth woven with carbon nanotubes is being used to make lightweight bulletproof vests. Another type of material woven with carbon nanotubes is being used to cover operating room mattresses. The unique electrical conductivity of

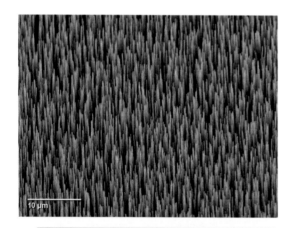

The forest of carbon nanotubes that make up a flame-resistant coating developed by scientists at the National Institute of Standards and Technology can be seen when viewed under a powerful microscope.

the nanotubes ensures that the charges in defibrillators stay safely grounded, protecting the patients, doctors, and other operating room staff. A Belgian company also makes anti-static clothing for people who work in microelectronics manufacturing so that the workers do not carry dangerous electric charges.

Scientists at the National Institute of Standards and Technology (NIST) have also developed a coating made from carbon nanotubes that greatly reduces the flammability of the foam that is used in furniture. Widespread use of such a coating could help lessen the threat of fires in homes and business, potentially saving many lives. Scientists in this field are currently working on materials that can act as filters for toxic gases in the air and for disease-causing agents, such as bacteria and viruses. The development of these materials could be very important to firefighters, emergency personal, members of the military, and hospital staff, as well as to ordinary citizens.

If you have an interest in developing unique materials that can enhance or save lives, you might look into the textile industry. Some of the job titles you might be interested in include textile chemist, chemical engineer, textile engineer, or textile laboratory technician.

FROM LABORATORY TO LIFE

Environmental scientists are looking into nanomaterials to filter harmful viruses, bacteria, and toxic

ITTY-BITTY BEAUTY

Maybe you've seen pictures of white-nosed sunbathers on the beach. The white paste on their nose is zinc oxide, and it is a sunscreen. The days of snow-white noses have disappeared, possibly forever, because scientists have discovered that zinc oxide paste turns into a silky-smooth clear substance when it is broken down into nanoparticles.

Sunscreens are not the only cosmetic substances that use nanoparticles. Makers of anti-aging skin creams say that the nanoparticles in their products slip between the cells in the outer layer of skin to get directly to the lower layer of skin where new skin cells are made. They claim that the nanoparticles are carrying vitamin A, which is believed to help diminish the appearance of wrinkles. Other skin care creams contain nanoparticles that kill bacteria, decreasing the likelihood of acne breakouts.

Most cosmetic scientists, including those working with nanotechnology, have chemistry degrees, but other science degrees, such as chemical engineering and biology, are viable options as well.

chemicals from contaminated water in the hopes of providing clean drinking water for everyone. Agricultural scientists are investigating nanomaterials as well. Some of these materials can absorb a lot of moisture, which means scientists may be able to impregnate them with pesticides, nutrient solutions, or growth hormones. They can then be planted

A factory worker assembles a food wrapping film that incorporates nanotechnology to prevent the infiltration of bacteria, moisture, household chemicals, and other harmful substances into food.

alongside the seeds in the field. Agronomists and crop scientists are also exploring nanoparticles that migrate to specific plant parts and then release the chemicals, such as nutrients, that they carry. Genes may be delivered to specific parts of the plant in this way, too.

Food scientists are in the process of developing nanoscale additives that could make low-fat foods tastier. They are also investigating the addition of vitamins and fish oils to a variety of food products. Food safety engineers are exploring packaging options that can detect the presence of pathogens in food. In the future, they hope to develop packaging that would warn consumers that the product is beginning to spoil. The reduction in food waste will become more important as the population of the world grows and farmers struggle to feed everyone.

Along with the job titles already mentioned, plant pathologists, food science technicians, and food safety technicians are likely to be on the cutting-edge of nanotechnology in the food industry.

TO CATCH A CROOK

Most nanotechnology applications in the forensic sciences are still in the experimental phase, but they are getting closer to being used in the field every day. The most developed application so far is in the area of fingerprinting. Similar to current fingerprinting powders, nanoparticles bind to a fingerprint pattern and make it visible. Because nanoparticles are much smaller, however, they can produce a more detailed image of the print—a characteristic that can be very useful when the fingerprints are old or faint. Scientists are also experimenting with fluorescent nanoparticles, which would make fingerprint development even easier.

In the future, forensic scientists hope to use nanotechnology to reveal yet more clues. Some of the areas they are working on include nanoparticles that detect specific chemicals in sweat—the break down products of cocaine or nicotine, for example—and faster, less expensive, portable DNA testing kits. The FBI, CIA, and local law enforcement agencies all employ forensic chemists and forensic science technicians.

CHAPTER FOUR

NUTS AND BOLTS:
NANOMACHINES

anufacturing at the nanoscale is increasingly used to create new materials, structures, devices, and systems. Nanomanufacturing can take place in one of two ways—top-down or bottom-up. Top-down manufacturing means reducing large-scale materials to nanoscale. Bottom-up manufacturing involves building materials from atomic- or molecular-scale components. Building materials atom by atom or molecule by molecule involves less waste but can be time consuming. Researchers are exploring the possibilities of grouping certain molecular-scale components that can "self-assemble," meaning that they spontaneously create an ordered structure. Nanomaterials often have unique and useful properties. They may be stronger, lighter, more durable, or electrically conductive. Some nanomaterials repel water or are anti-reflective or ultraviolet- or infrared-resistant. Others are self-cleaning or have anti-fog, antimicrobial, or scratch-resistant properties. Job opportunities exist in the automotive, aeronautical, robotic, and electronics industries, as well as many others.

The Quant F sports car, made by nanoFlowCELL AG in Lichtenstein, uses the flow cell technology of electrolyte fuel instead of lithium-ion technology. Scientists working for automobile manufacturers have used their knowledge of nanotechnology to create sustainable methods for storing electricity and develop materials that help keep cars dirt and dent free.

LAND, SEA, AND AIR

Nanomaterials were first used in the automobile industry in 2002. One of the largest current uses in this field is the addition of super-strong nanofibers to plastic to create strong, light-weight car bumpers that resist denting and scratching. Nano-engineered polishes and paints are also being used to keep cars and trucks looking

SEEING AT NANOSCALE

The microscopes needed to manipulate things on the nanoscale were invented relatively recently—about thirty years ago. The scanning tunneling microscope (STM) was developed by a research team at IBM led by Gerd Binnig and Heinrich Rohrer in 1981. The STM was the first microscope that really allowed scientists to work on the nanoscale. While its main function was to measure minute particles, it could also move tiny objects, such as atoms. The first

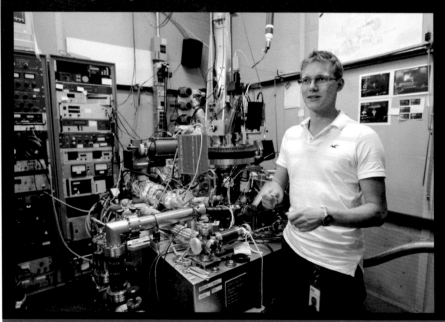

A nanoscale researcher employed by IBM stands next to a scanning tunneling microscope (STM). Scientists at the company developed the first STM in 1981.

example of manipulating materials on the atomic level took place on November 11, 1989, when Don Eigler and his colleagues spelled out the IBM logo in atoms. To do this, the researchers moved thirty-five xenon atoms around on a background of copper atoms to spell out the letters IBM. In 2009, Hari Manoharan, Christopher Moon, and students at Stanford's physics department topped this feat by writing Stanford's initials in letters smaller than an atom, demonstrating the possibilities of even denser information storage in the future.

shiny and new by repelling road grime and resisting the fading power of ultraviolet (UV) rays from the sun. Some automobile manufacturers are also using glass coated in a one-atom thick film of graphite, which makes it self-cleaning, in windshields and side mirrors. The shipping industry uses a super-slick nano-enabled paint that allows ships to cut smoothly through the water. Barnacles will not grow on the paint, and it is also resistant to damage from UV rays and corrosive salt spray. The aerospace industry is also interested in developing more nano-enabled composites that could result in stronger, lighter aircraft and spacecraft. Lighter aircraft would mean less fuel would be needed, potentially saving money as well as the environment.

Job opportunities in these fields include those for mechanical engineers, materials scientists, solid state chemists, electrical systems engineers, and electrical and mechanical engineering technicians.

CUTTING-EDGE ELECTRONICS

The electronics arena is another exciting area of nanoscale research. Electronics include everything from computers and flat-screen televisions to stereo components and cell phones. In the world of electronics, the semiconductor is king. Semiconductors lie at the heart of all digital devices. A semiconductor is a material that has electrical conductivity properties between those of a metal, which conducts electricity very well, and an insulator, like glass, that barely conducts electricity at all. The element silicon (Si) is a very useful semiconductor and has been used in electronics since the 1950s. Today, computer chips are filled with silicon-based transistors. A transistor is a tiny switch that can be turned on and off with an electric signal. Basically, by working together, the transistors tell a computer what to do.

Developers of digital devices are always in pursuit of smaller and smaller components. However, they seem to have reached a physical limit with silicon-based computer chips. Scientists and engineers working in the electronics field believe the next step is to replace today's silicon-based transistors with those made from carbon nanotubes. By doing this, they believe they will be able to engineer smaller, faster, more powerful, and more energy efficient computers that will have the potential to hold exponentially higher amounts of data than the computers that are available today. In 2013, engineers at Stanford University took a big step forward on this road to more

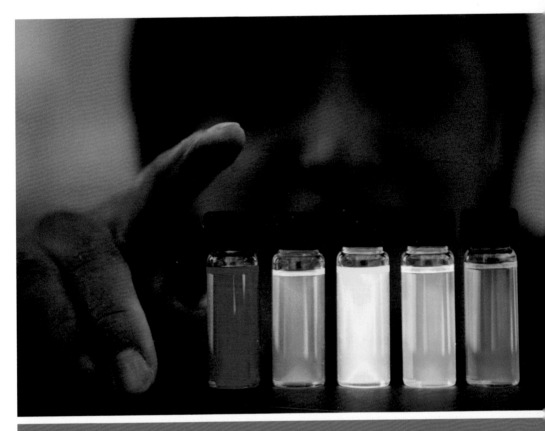

Semiconductor nanocrystals, called quantum dots, produce a dazzling rainbow of colors when viewed under ultraviolet light.

powerful computers by creating a fully functional device made entirely out of carbon nanotubes.

Computers are not the only electronic devices to take advantage of nanotechnology. Some of the flat-screen televisions released to the market for the first time in 2014 contained LEDs made of nanocrystals called quantum dots. Quantum dots range in size from 1 to 6 nanometers in diameter. Different sized dots emit a distinct wavelength of light. Larger dots tend to emit light on the red end of the visible light spectrum while the smaller dots emit light on the blue end. A rainbow of colors can be made just by changing the size of the dot. Like integrated chips in computers, quantum dots are made from a semiconductor, such as silicon or germanium (Ge).

Electronics engineers get their ideas from many places. The idea behind computer tablet screens that get bright in daylight, for example, was first developed by studying and understanding the iridescence exhibited by some animals, such as butterflies and peacocks. Iridescence is the property by which certain surfaces change color as the angle of viewing or the angle of illumination changes. By creating materials that could mimic that functionality, engineers could address the problem of reading a computer screen outdoors. The idea of emulating natural phenomenon to address human problems is called biomimicry.

The electronics industry is in great need of skilled workers who are interested in developing new and improved electronic devices. Training usually involves specialty schools that give students access to the equipment specifically used in electronics nanotechnology. Electronics technicians and those with associate's degrees in electronics engineering are important to the operation and repair of the robotics and electronic equipment that are needed to produce nanotechnology products. Electrical or electronics engineers with bachelor's, master's, and doctorate degrees generally focus more on the research and development of device design, tooling, and processes that are needed to make these devices.

CHAPTER FIVE

MINIATURE MEDICINE

Much of what goes on inside the human body naturally occurs at the nanoscale. A strand of DNA, for example, is about 2 nanometers in diameter. Hemoglobin, a protein that carries oxygen throughout the body, is 5.5 nanometers in diameter. So, in a way, life itself is nature's nanotechnology.

MEDICAL MARVELS

One of the most exciting fields currently under development is the use of nanotechnology in medicine. The potential to use nanosensors and nanoscale robots to diagnose and treat disease is especially promising. Scientists at Scripps Health and Caltech have developed a biosensor that is much smaller than a grain of sand. This nanosensor could be injected into a patient's bloodstream to monitor his or her glucose levels. The use of this type of biosensor could greatly improve the quality of life for people with diabetes. Currently, a person with diabetes must prick a finger several times each day to draw a drop of blood that can then be placed into a glucose monitor to measure his or her blood sugar level. An internal biosensor could eliminate the need for these painful finger sticks. The

Thin, flexible, lightweight sensor systems could one day change the way doctors gather information about a patient's health.

biosensor works by detecting glucose molecules in the bloodstream. When it detects too much or too little glucose, the biosensor can send an alert to the patient's smartphone or other wireless device, letting the person know it is time for his or her medication or that medical attention should be sought. This biosensor is now being used to monitor glucose levels in animals. If the animal studies go well, human trials should follow.

Researchers who work in the laboratories of pharmaceutical companies are diligently searching for ways to attach medications to nanoparticles, potentially allowing targeted drug delivery within a patient's body.

Researchers at North Carolina State University are working to take this type of biosensor one step further. They have developed an injectable network of biosensors that not only can monitor glucose levels but can also automatically secrete insulin to regulate blood sugar. Their system is currently being tested in mice and has successfully maintained blood glucose levels in type 1 diabetic mice for up to ten days. Although these biosensors are programmed to detect glucose, researchers believe that similar sensors could be used to detect heart attacks before they happen, to track autoimmune diseases, to screen for rejection in organ donation, and possibly to detect cancer.

Another area of ongoing research includes the use of gold nanoshells in the diagnosis and treatment of cancer. A gold nanoshell is a spherical nanoparticle covered in a thin layer of gold. These nanoshells have different characteristics depending on their size. They may, for example, have different melting points, individual capacities to carry an electrical current, and disparate colors. Researchers have found that they can coat gold nanoshells with antibodies. Antibodies are proteins with the ability to recognize foreign particles in the body. They are very important to the immune system. The use of antibodies allows the gold nanoshells to recognize and adhere to cancer cells. If researchers attach a fluorescent marker to the gold nanoshells, these particles can show the location of a cancerous tumor, providing medical professionals with a powerful diagnostic tool. Scientists are also investigating the idea of using the gold nanoshells to destroy cancer cells. If a laser is directed at the area where the gold nanoshells have gathered, the gold heats up, essentially cooking the cancer cells without harming the surrounding healthy tissue. Researchers have also successfully produced nanoshells that can deliver chemotherapy drugs directly to cancer cells, specifically targeting them for destruction. So far, this research is limited to the laboratory, but the researchers' next step is to try their procedures in mice.

Medical researchers are also studying the possibilities of using nanosized robots to perform precision surgery in sensitive areas, such as the eye. Scientists believe that such a robot could be used to deliver specific drug doses or to help dissolve blood clots in the vessels of the eye, a common cause of lost vision. So far, they have successfully created a microbot that is about 285 micrometers in diameter. This microbot is magnetically directed and is currently being tested in rabbits. Research is ongoing to make the robots smaller.

Nanotechnology could also be the key to the diagnosis and treatment of disease in developing countries. In many areas of the world, a lack of medical facilities with proper equipment, such as refrigerators, makes diagnosis and treatment of disease extremely challenging. To help solve this problem, a U.S.-based company called Micronics Corporation, in conjunction with researchers at the University of Washington, has developed a credit card–sized disease-detecting kit called the DxBox. Using dried testing chemicals and nanosized tubes on the face of the card, doctors can perform blood tests to detect diseases such as malaria and tuberculosis, which kill millions of people around the world every year, without the need for expensive testing reagents or refrigeration.

These are only a few of the ongoing projects already in progress in the field of medical nanotechnology. There are many, many more, and experts predict the number of applications in the medical field will increase exponentially in the years to come. In the future, the need for medical technicians who can carry out studies and procedures to test the effectiveness and safety of developing nanomedicine is likely to increase by many

NANO SAFETY

Some people are concerned with the potential safety risks of a world laced with nanoparticles and nanotubes. One concern is the possibility of nanoparticles leaching into the human body from nano-enabled clothing and cosmetics. Toxicologists are not very concerned about silver, in particular, because it is not highly toxic to humans. However, other nanoparticles have not been as well studied.

Scientists have found that spherical fullerenes in the water accumulate in the brains and gills of fish. A fullerene is a generic term for a hollow sphere, tube, or other shape made of carbon atoms. Carbon nanotubes are one type of fullerene. Spherical fullerenes are sometimes called buckyballs, too. The accumulation of the fullerenes in the fish was not conclusively harmful, but research is ongoing.

Other studies have shown that when rats inhale carbon nanotubes, the fullerenes lodge in the animals' lungs much like asbestos does. Asbestos is a known carcinogen, or cancer-causing agent, in humans. Researchers found that the rats developed mesothelioma, the same type of cancer caused by the inhalation of asbestos. It is unknown whether or not carbon nanotubes will do the same in humans. There have been no reports of nanotechnology workers being harmed by the nanoparticles they work with, but scientists are studying the situation to determine where the most likely dangers lie.

times what it is today. In addition, biologists, biochemists, and other medical researchers who have the educational background and skill set to work in this promising field will be in high demand.

HEALTHY HELPERS

Medicine is not the only place where the use of nanotechnology has the potential to help save human lives. Scientists are also investigating its use for environmental monitoring and remediation. In 2010, scientists from the

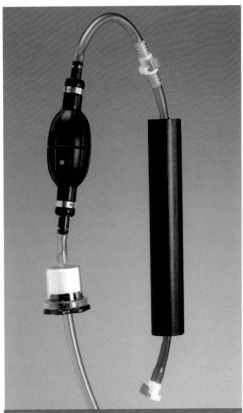

The shortage of clean drinking water is a serious problem in developing nations. Portable filters, such as this prototype containing carbon nanotubes, could one day provide a simple, inexpensive solution.

United Nations estimated that more people die worldwide from the lack of fresh drinking water than from all types of violence, including war. Environmental scientists have found that filters infused with nanoparticles and nanomagnets can filter out unwanted or harmful chemicals, leaving behind fresh drinking water. Carbon nanotubes can be made large enough to allow water molecules through but not large enough for pollutant molecules. Nanomagnets can filter out magnetic particles, such as excess iron. Other types of nanoparticles are attractive to pollutants such as arsenic and can filter out those harmful substances. Filters can also be made to separate out salt particles from seawater, leaving behind fresh, clean drinking water. Degrees and specialty studies in environmental science, hydrology, and environmental engineering would lead to this type of career.

CHAPTER SIX

INTERESTED IN THE INFINITESIMAL?

As previously mentioned, most nanotechnology jobs do not come with a handy label such as "nanotechnologist." Instead, companies that hire people with expertise in nanotechnology may be looking for a microfabrication engineer, a drug delivery scientist, a medical device engineer, a near field semiconductor engineer, an engineering technician, a laboratory technologist, or a research scientist. They may even be looking for a business or a project manager. Once you decide on an area you are specifically interested in, you can begin to ask people their job titles.

THE NEED FOR NANOTECHS

To apply for a nanotechnology job or internship, you will most likely need a résumé or curriculum vitae. A résumé is a general and concise introduction of your experiences and skills as it relates to a particular job opening. As such, a résumé should be tailored to a specific position. In contrast, a curriculum vitae (CV) is a fairly detailed description of your academic accomplishments. In general, a résumé is more suitable for applying for a position in business or industry, where a CV is more appropriate for use in a position in academia or research.

Some nanotechnology workers conduct their research within "clean" rooms, which are controlled environments free of contaminants such as dust, airborne microbes, and chemical vapors. The workers' suits prevent hair and skin particles from being shed within the clean room environment.

Résumés are usually no more than one page in length and are generally accompanied by a cover letter. A résumé should include your name and contact information, education, and work experience. Remember, a résumé should be concise. Therefore, try to avoid paragraphs and use bulleted sentences that begin with action verbs. Tweak your résumé to make the most relevant experience for the particular job stand out. Do not worry if you have never held a paying job in your field. To show employers that you have relevant experience, include internships, work/study experiences, volunteer positions, extracurricular activities, and any other unpaid experiences that specifically relate to your goals.

Your cover letter should be brief and explain why you are sending your résumé. Research the company before you write your cover letter. Include details that show you know something about the company—what it does, what its needs are, or why you are interested in working for it. Each cover letter should be unique to the company and the position you are applying for. Do not send a form letter. Be sure to address your cover letter to the specific person listed in the job posting. If a specific person is not named in the job listing, try searching the company's website for the director of human resources. Résumés and cover letters demonstrate your writing skills so make sure to proofread them before you send them.

The most important thing to remember about sending your résumé and cover letter is to follow the employer's directions. If the job posting asks that

Research each company and position you are interested in and use the knowledge you obtain to focus your résumé and create a unique cover letter for each specific company and position.

A SAMPLE RÉSUMÉ

Mary Smith
123 Bay Street
Shreveport, LA 71101
(555) 333-2300
mary.smith@email.com

OBJECTIVE

An internship or a cooperative education experience in nanosystems engineering

EDUCATION

Shreveport High School, Class of 2013 (3.5 GPA)
Louisiana Tech University
Bachelor of science in nanosystems engineering, May 2017
Major GPA: 3.35   Current Class Level: Senior
Relevant Coursework: Nanosystems and Devices, Nanosystems Modeling, Advanced Materials for Nanosystems, Solid State Electronics

TECHNICAL PROJECTS, LABS, AND RESEARCH

Nanowire Design
Theorized, designed, and tested new nanowire fabrication technology for senior design project.
Research Paper on Nanowire Technology
Analysis of nanowire potential in the semiconductor industry. Paper accepted and presented at nanotechnology conference, Anaheim, CA, May 2015.

TECHNICAL SKILLS

Equipment: CNC machine, lathes, mills, scanning electron microscope
Computer: SolidWorks, Pro-Engineer, Microsoft Word/Excel/PowerPoint

COMMUNITY SERVICE AND INVOLVEMENT

Society for Nanosystems Engineering Students at Louisiana State University, President
FIRST Robotics Competition Champion, Team Leader

EXPERIENCE

Research Assistant
Scanning Electron Microscope Laboratory, Louisiana Tech University
January 2015–present
Responsible for the preparation and imaging of biological specimens, preparation of chemical solutions, and general laboratory maintenance.
Clean Room Maintenance
Institute for Nanosystems, Baton Rouge, LA, June 2014–December 2015
Performed cleaning and maintenance for two Class-1000 clean rooms.

you send your documents by e-mail, you will usually be given instructions on whether to send them in the body of the e-mail or as an attachment. If asked to send your résumé in the body of the e-mail, copy and paste your résumé into your e-mail message. Use a basic font, such as Times New Roman, and remove all the formatting. If the job posting asks that you to send your résumé as an attachment, attach a Microsoft Word or Adobe PDF file to your e-mail message. If the job posting does not specify, sending your documents in the body of your e-mail may help keep you out of the company's spam folder.

SHOWCASING YOUR SKILLS

If the experiences and skills detailed in your résumé or CV catch the eye of the person who is hiring, chances are you will be asked to participate in an interview. Prior to your interview, research the company as much as possible. Prepare a list of questions to ask. In addition, practice answering some of the more common interview questions. This preparation can help relieve stress on interview day. For example, you may be asked to tell the interviewer about yourself. Practice a response that will tell him or her how your education and experiences connect with the skills needed to carry out the job you are interviewing for.

For an in-person interview, you should dress professionally and allow plenty of time to reach the place where your interview will be held. Clean, press, and

At left is an example of a résumé for an internship or a cooperative education opportunity in nanosystems engineering. A successful résumé clearly details the applicant's experience, skills, and qualities that can benefit an organization or company.

COMMON INTERVIEW QUESTIONS

You may want to practice your answers to some of the more common interview questions. The objective is not necessarily to memorize your answers word for word but to get comfortable with speaking your answers out loud to help you feel more confident on the day of the interview. As much as possible, try to connect each of your answers with the skills required for the specific job you are interviewing for.

1. Tell me about yourself.
2. What is your greatest professional strength?
3. Why did you choose this field?
4. Give an example of a difficult work situation or a major challenge you have faced and tell us how you overcame it.
5. Do you have any questions for us?

Questions you might want to ask a potential employer include:

1. Why is this position open?
2. Can you show me some examples of projects I'd be working on?

> 3. What are some of the challenges a person in this position might face?
> 4. What is a typical day or week like in this position?
> 5. When do you expect to make a decision on filling this position?

get your interview attire ready the night before. Try to arrive at least ten minutes early and use the extra time to review your notes. If possible, bring a brochure from your college or program that describes your courses, technical skills acquired, and specialized equipment used. If your program does not offer a brochure, make a list yourself for reference.

Whether your interview is in person or by phone, remember that your attitude and communication skills are just as important as your technical ones. Do not be afraid to ask questions of the

Presenting a confident, professional image will create a great first impression the day of your interview.

interviewers. In fact, asking questions shows that you are interested in the company and tends to build interest. You should also be prepared for multiple interviews. It is not uncommon to speak to three or four people during the interview process. You may also be called back for a second interview on another day. Do not forget to send a thank-you note after your interview.

NETWORKING IN NANO

Because nanotechnology is on the cutting-edge of science, your learning will not end with graduation from a certificate or college program. In this competitive global economy, the need to acquire new skills and update old ones will always be a vital part of your job. One way to find out more about what scientists and engineers in the specific area of nanotechnology you are interested in are exploring is to connect with them on social media sites, such as LinkedIn or Twitter. These social media sites can help you discover what nanotechnology students and graduates from all over the country are working on. By following undergraduates and alumni from colleges and universities as well as students involved in technical training, you can identify areas in which you wish to focus your life-long learning. You can also get information on current job postings and what the requirements are for each job. This knowledge will allow you to focus your future studies on areas that will tell you more about the specific career you are interested in. Social media sites can also alert you to professional organizations that you may want to explore for further information.

CHAPTER SEVEN

THE SHAPE OF THINGS TO COME

It's hard to know where nanotechnology might take the world in the future. Remember that only two hundred years ago, televisions, airplanes, personal computers, cell phones, lasers, and rockets did not exist. With the help of nanotechnology, advances in robotics, prosthetics, and better communication are definitely on the way. As science advances, the world is sure to look quite different in another two hundred years.

BIG BUILT FROM LITTLE

Imagine a skyscraper taller than ever before or building shapes that are not possible using today's materials. In the future, scientists believe the invention of super-strong nanomaterials will allow these things to become reality. Engineers may even be able to construct an elevator to take people and supplies into space. The proposed space elevator would be made of a carbon nanotube composite ribbons that would stretch approximately 62,000 miles (100,000 km) into space. The ribbon would serve as a track for elevator cars. This idea is not as far-fetched as it seems. Carbon nanotubes have

61

An artist made this rendering of one of the many possible designs for a future space elevator. The space elevator has a carbon nanotube ribbon that stretches from Earth to a counterweight in space.

the potential to be 100 times stronger than steel and they are as flexible as plastic. Scientists believe that carbon nanotubes and materials like them will eventually allow humans to build structures we have never even thought of before.

Back down on Earth, new discoveries in nanotechnology could also help engineers design and build more efficient solar cells, affordable hydrogen cells, and better cooling mechanisms that could be used for nuclear fusion reactors. All of these applications would decrease human reliance on nonrenewable energy sources, such as fossil fuels.

Scientists envision other endeavors to protect the planet, too. Nanogrids that can utilize the energy from the sun to break down oil spills and leave behind biodegradable compounds, for example. Or the utilization of new nanomaterials to make small, inexpensive water filters that can remove antibiotics from our water supply.

Protecting human health and life is also high on the priority list. Researchers are working on a nanofiber mesh that can absorb toxins in the blood. They hope to use this fabric one day to provide inexpensive, compact blood filtration systems to people who suffer from kidney failure. Other medical advances may include using carbon nanotubes as a foundation to grow human body parts, nanoparticles that deliver drugs and other materials to diseased areas of the body, or nanobots that can carry out complex, delicate surgeries inside the body.

Researchers are also working on improving the technology and tools other scientists need to make nanoscale products. This includes a desktop fabrication tool that allows scientists to create structures in nanoscale. It also

An engineer works on a piece of equipment that incorporates a high-resolution scanning electron microscope with ultra-precision tooling that enables the assembly of atoms and molecules into nanostructures.

includes designing and building nanoscale motors and batteries that can be used in other products.

THE FUTURE OF NANOTECH

Whether your interest lies in saving or improving lives, cleaning up and protecting the environment,

FROM FANTASTIC FICTION TO FANTASTIC FUTURES

Authors of science fiction novels often envision our world as a very different place. Sometime, though, their imaginations are not so far off. In 1969, science fiction author John Brunner predicted the advent of on-demand television, the invention of the laser printer, and the organization of the European Union in his book titled *Stand on Zanzibar*. Today, all of these things are a reality. In *Cyborg*, published in 1972, author Martin Caidin imagined that one day bionic limbs would be available. In 2003, a thirteen-year-old cancer patient received the first bionic leg implant. William Gibson envisioned cyberspace and computer hackers in his 1984 publication *Neuromancer*. Today people often hear news reports about the latest cyber-attacks on corporate targets or other victims.

Many other authors and screenwriters have imagined our future with nanotechnology. Some of these include the movies *Fantastic Voyage* (1966), *Inner Space* (1987), and *Honey I Shrunk the Kids* (1989). Although scientists have yet to shrink a human down to nanoscale, they have certainly shrunk other things. Other science fiction authors envision a time when nanobots develop the ability to reproduce outside of the laboratory, run amok,

(continued on the next page)

(continued from the previous page)

and consume everything in sight. This situation is the basis of the so-called "grey goo" nightmare and the impetus of plots such as the evil, shape-shifting killer robot in *Terminator 2* (1991) and the nanite infestation on the television series *Star Trek: The Next Generation* ("Evolution" episode, aired in 1989). Books—such as *Decipher* by Stel Pavlou (2001), *Prey* by Michael Crichton (2002), and *The Lazarus Vendetta* by Robert Ludlum (2005)—also envision what might happen in a fully nano-enabled world.

or improving communication, nanotechnology is the future. If you'd like to be part of this cutting-edge, exciting field, consider focusing on developing your understanding of the underlying scientific concepts and practicing your hands-on design and building skills. Your knowledge and skills could end up turning science fiction into science fact.

One day, everybody may be wearing "smart clothes" made with cloth that contains tiny, flexible nanocomputers. Not only will electronic devices be woven into clothing, but scientists envision cloth that will have electronic capabilities of its own. The idea is to use such cloth to monitor body functions, such as heart rate, blood pressure, and other medically important statistics.

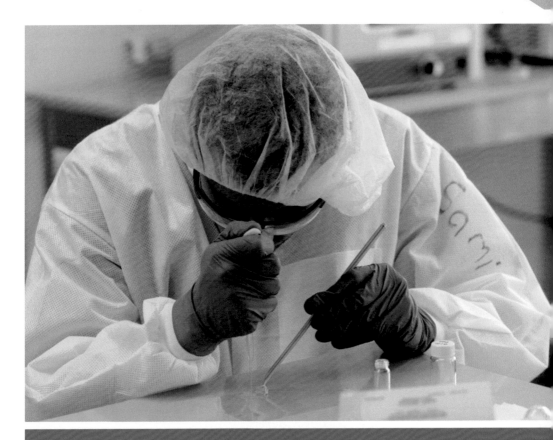

The future uses of nanoparticles are immeasurable. Companies and research institutions will require many highly trained, creative, and knowledgeable workers to take full advantage of this technology.

"Smart clothing" would require "smart batteries." Some experts imagine sweaters sprayed with solar cells that could charge a cell phone or other electronic devices, including the sweater itself.

What if scientists could make a nanocomputer the size of a human cell that could be implanted into the brain? Combat pilots could be linked to their plane's computers, making weapons easier to control and more accurate. Implantable computers could hold a library's worth of information, making the person super-smart. OK, that capability may still be a little too far off into the future. But what if you could have your own invisibility cloak? That one is not as far off as it seems. Scientists at Duke University have recently ascertained how to use nanoparticles to redirect light around an object, rendering it invisible. Although their primary focus at the moment is on products for the military, maybe, one day, you'll be able to buy your very own invisibility cloak. Perhaps you could even help them perfect it.

GLOSSARY

accredited Formally recognized for its specific standards, such as for a course of study or an organization.

antibody A protein capable of recognizing foreign substances in the blood.

biomimicry The imitation of natural phenomena in designs produced to solve complex human problems.

buckyball A hollow ball made up of carbon atoms.

carbon nanotubes A hollow tube made from a rolled-up sheet of carbon atoms.

carcinogen A substance that causes cancer in humans.

conductor A substance, such as a metal, that conducts electricity well.

curriculum vitae A detailed overview of academic accomplishments, including awards, publications, and academic memberships.

engineering The application of science and mathematics to the design and construction of products that solve human problems.

fullerene A generic term that applies to any hollow structure made of carbon atoms.

grey goo scenario A scenario in which nanosized robots develop the ability to reproduce outside of the laboratory and destroy the world.

insulator A substance, such as glass, that does not conduct electricity.

interdisciplinary Involving two or more academic or scientific disciplines.

iridescence The property in which certain surfaces change color as the angle of viewing or the angle of illumination changes.

macroscopic Something that is big enough to be seen by the naked eye.

matter Anything that has mass and takes up space.

nanoparticle A particle whose size can be measured in billionths of a meter.

quantum dot A nanoparticle of semiconductor material that changes colors based on its size.

remediation The act or process of correcting or counteracting a problem.

résumé A concise introduction of experiences and skills as they relate to a specific career or position.

semiconductor A substance with electrical conductivity properties between that of a conductor and an insulator.

transistor Tiny switches that can be turned on and off by electric signals that are used to control electronic devices.

FOR MORE INFORMATION

For Inspiration and Recognition of Science and
    Technology (FIRST)
200 Bedford Street
Manchester, NH 03101
(603) 666-3906
Website: http://www.usfirst.org
FIRST operates the Junior FIRST LEGO League, the FIRST
    LEGO League, and the FIRST Robotics and FIRST Tech
    Challenge competitions.

International Council on Nanotechnology (ICON)
Rice University
MS 63
P.O. Box 1892
Houston, TX 77251-1892
(713) 348-8211
Website: http://icon.rice.edu/newsroom.cfm
ICON sponsors forums and events to explore the health
    and environmental risks of nanotechnology and ways
    to minimize those risks while maximizing societal
    benefit.

Nanotechnology Applications and Career Knowledge
    (NACK) Network
Website: http://nano4me.org
The NACK Network offers live webinars, videotaped
    interviews, and a list of alumni that provides examples
    of the jobs they do and the types of experiences listed
    on their résumés.

National Institute for Nanotechnology (NINT)
11421 Saskatchewan Drive
Edmonton, AB T6G 2M9
Canada
(780) 641-1600
Website: http://nint-innt.ca
The NINT provides information about cutting-edge nano-
technology projects in Canada.

National Nanotechnology Infrastructure Network (NNIN)
250 Duffield Hall, Cornell University
Ithaca, NY 14853-2700
(607) 255-2329
Website: http://www.nnin.org/research-experience
-undergraduates
The NNIN is a network of fourteen nanotechnology
centers around the United States that provides
hands-on training in nanotechnology and offers a
very successful research program for undergraduate students.

National Nanotechnology Initiative (NNI)
4201 Wilson Boulevard
Stafford II Room 405
Arlington, VA 22230
(703) 292-8626
Website: http://www.nano.gov
The NNI is the U.S. government's research and development initiative in nanotechnology. Its website provides
a link to the online science magazine *Nanooze*, as
well as a list of certificate programs and college and
university courses of study.

U.S. Bureau of Labor Statistics (BLS)
Postal Square Building
2 Massachusetts Avenue NE
Washington, DC 20212-0001
(202) 691-5200
Website: http://www.bls.gov
The Bureau of Labor Statistics publishes *The Occupational Outlook Handbook. The Occupational Outlook Handbook* offers information on hundreds of jobs, including their responsibilities, the type of work environment, the education and training needed, salary information, and whether or not the occupation is expected to grow in the future.

Youth Science Canada
1550 Kingston Road, Suite 213
Pickering, ON L1V 1C3
Canada
(416) 341-0040
Website: https://www.youthscience.ca
Youth Science Canada provides project-based science challenges through local, regional, and national science fairs.

WEBSITES

Because of the changing nature of Internet links, Rosen Publishing has developed an online list of websites related to the subject of this book. This site is updated regularly. Please use this link to access the list:

http://www.rosenlinks.com/PTC/Nano

FOR FURTHER READING

Berger, Sandra. *The Best Summer Programs for Teens: America's Top Classes, Camps, and Courses for College-Bound Students*. Waco, TX: Prufrock Press, 2013.

Berlatsky, Noah, ed. *Nanotechnology* (Opposing Viewpoints). Detroit, MI: Greenhaven Press, 2014.

Boysen, Earl, and Nancy Muir. *Nanotechnology for Dummies*. Hoboken, NJ: Wiley Publishing, 2011.

Cook, Robin. *Nano*. New York, NY: Berkley Publishing Group, 2013.

Heinrichs, Ann. *Nanotechnologist* (Cool Science Careers). Ann Arbor, MI: Cherry Lake Publishing, 2014.

Kleinberg, Suzanne. *From Playstation to Workstation: A Career Guide for Generation Text*. Toronto, ON: Potential to Soar, 2011.

McCray, W. Patrick. *The Visioneers: How a Group of Elite Scientists Pursued Space Colonies, Nanotechnologies, and a Limitless Future*. Princeton, NJ: Princeton University Press, 2013.

Peterson's. *Teen's Guide to College & Career Planning*. Lawrenceville, NJ: Peterson's, 2011.

Porter, London. *Rockstar Your Job Interview*. New York, NY: 73 Publishing, 2013.

Rogers, Ben, Jesse Adams, and Sumita Pennathur. *Nanotechnology: The Whole Story*. Boca Raton, FL: CRC Press, 2013.

Yate, Martin. *Knock 'em Dead: Secrets & Strategies for First-Time Job Seekers*. Holbrook, MA: Adams Media, 2013.

BIBLIOGRAPHY

Bello, Mark. "Layered Security: Carbon Nanotubes Promise Improved Flame-Resistant Coating." *NIST Tech Beat*, January 14, 2014. Retrieved September 24, 2014 (http://www.nist.gov/el/fire_research/flame-011414.cfm).

Boychuk, Evelyn. "Silver Nanoparticle Use Spurs U.S. Consumer Database." CBC News, November 8, 2013. Retrieved September 24, 2014 (http://www.cbc.ca/news/technology/silver-nanoparticle-use-spurs-u-s-consumer-database-1.2415424).

Cave, Holly. "Nanomedicines Set to Revolutionise the Treatment of Diabetes." *The Guardian.* Retrieved September 24, 2014 (http://www.theguardian.com/what-is-nano/nanomedicines-revolutionise-treatment-diabetes).

Chan, Chi. "From Nanotech to Nanoscience." *Chemical Heritage Magazine.* Retrieved September 20, 2014 (http://www.chemheritage.org/discover/media/magazine/articles/26-2-from-nanotech-to-nanoscience.aspx).

Corcoran, Emily, ed. "Sick Water? The Central Role of Wastewater Management in Sustainable Development." United Nations Environment Programme, UN-HABITAT, GRID-Arendal. 2010. Retrieved September 24, 2014 (http://www.unep.org/pdf/SickWater_screen.pdf).

Drexler, Eric. "How to Study for a Career in Nanotechnology." *Metamodern*, February 24, 2010. Retrieved September 15, 2014 (http://metamodern.com/

2010/02/24/how-to-study-for-a-career-in
-nanotechnology).

Forbes, Peter. "Self-Cleaning Materials: Lotus Leaf-Induced
Nanotechnology." *Scientific American*, August
2008. Retrieved September 24, 2014 (http://www
.scientificamerican.com/article/self-cleaning-materials).

Halford, Bethany. "Nanotech Makes Your Brown Eyes
Blue." *Chemical & Engineering News*, October 10,
2005. Retrieved September 21, 2014 (http://pubs.
acs.org/cen/science/83/8341sci2.html).

Hubbard, Bethany. "A Knack for Nanoscience: An Interview with Dr. Amanda Petford-Long." *Helix Magazine*,
December 5, 2013. Retrieved September 28, 2014
(https://helix.northwestern.edu/article/knack
-nanoscience).

Kullman, Joe. "Nanotechnology and Society: An Interview with David Guston." *Research Matters*, August
13, 2009. Retrieved October 3, 2014 (http://
researchmatters.asu.edu/stories/nanotechnology
-and-society-interview-david-guston-1275).

Lovgren, Stefan. "Spray-On Solar-Power Cells Are True
Breakthrough." *National Geographic*, January
14, 2005. Retrieved September 24, 2014 (http://
news.nationalgeographic.com/news/2005/01/
0114_050114_solarplastic.html).

Luna, Taryn. "Reebok, MC10 Tackle Head Injures with
Device." *Boston Globe*, June 16, 2014. Retrieved
September 29, 2014 (http://www.bostonglobe.com/
business/2014/06/14/reebok-develop-device
-monitor-athletes-for-head-injuries/lePeOZTLXg7
1u2KN4Te7MK/story.html).

Lundquist, Brain. "Interview with Dr. Eric Drexler." *Nanotechnology Now*, December 26, 2013. Retrieved October 3, 2014 (http://www.nanotech-now.com/columns/?article=832).

National Nanotechnology Infrastructure Network. "Nanotechnology Careers: Is a Career in Nanotechnology in Your Future?" Retrieved August 19, 2014 (http://www.nnin.org/news-events/spotlights/nanotechnology-careers).

Newmarker, Chris. "Innovega Putting a Lens onto Device Innovation." *Qmed*, January 7, 2014. Retrieved September 24, 2014 (http://www.qmed.com/mpmn/medtechpulse/innovega-putting-lens-device-innovation).

PhysOrg. "Nano World: Invisibility through Nano." May 25, 2006. Retrieved September 24, 2014 (http://phys.org/news67787896.html).

Roco, Mihail, Chad Mirkin, and Mark Hersam. "Nanotechnology Research Directions for Societal Needs in 2012: Summary of International Study." *Journal of Nanoparticle Research*, January 30, 2011. Retrieved September 11, 2014 (http://www.nsf.gov/crssprgm/nano/reports/MCR_11-0301_Nanotechnology_Research_Directions_To_2020_JNR13.pdf).

Stober, Dan. "Reading the Fine Print Takes On a New Meaning." *Stanford Report*, January 28, 2009. Retrieved September 18, 2014 (http://news.stanford.edu/news/2009/january28/small-012809.html).

INDEX

I

interviewing, 57–60

M

Manoharan, Hari, 41
MathCounts, 24, 27
McLellan, William, 15
medicine, nanotechnology and,
    8, 45–51, 63
Moon, Christopher, 41

N

nanometer, explanation of, 11
nanotechnology
    explanation of, 8
    future of, 61–68
    preparing for career in, 18–19,
        20–26
    safety of, 50–51
    significant events in, 22–23
National Nanotechnology
    Infrastructure Network
    (NNIN), 24
networking, 60
Neuromancer, 65
Newman, Thomas, 16

Q

quantum dots, 43–44

R

résumé, 26, 53–57
Rohrer, Heinrich, 40

S

scanning tunneling microscope,
    22, 40
scholarships, 27–29
science fairs, 25
Science Olympiad, 24, 26
shipping industry, nanotechnology
    and, 41
Stand on Zanzibar, 65
STEM, explanation of, 24

T

textile industry, nanotechnology
    and, 8, 12–13, 30–33,
    66–67
Thermo Scientific Pierce
    Scholarship Program,
    27–29
top-down manufacturing, 38

V

volunteer work, 26

ABOUT THE AUTHOR

Kristi Lew has written more than forty books for teachers and young people. Fascinated with science from a young age, she studied biochemistry and genetics in college. Before becoming a full-time science writer, she worked in genetics laboratories and taught high school science. When she's not writing, she can often be found sailing or kayaking around the Gulf of Mexico or out on the back deck with her nose buried in a book finding out what's new in the world of science.

PHOTO CREDITS

Cover Alexander Raths/Shutterstock.com; cover (background), back cover, p. 1 Mopic/Shutterstock.com; pp. 5, 46 Yoshikazu Tsuno/AFP/Getty Images; p. 9 Peter Menzel/Science Source; p. 12 York Minster, Yorkshire, UK/Bridgeman Images; p. 14 Pacific Northwest National Laboratory, U.S. Department of Energy; p. 18 © Bill Aron/PhotoEdit; p. 20 Jan Woitas/DPA/Landov; pp. 21, 27, 43, 54 © AP Images; p. 25 Tim Sloan/AFP/Getty Images; pp. 31, 51 SSPL/Getty Images; p. 32 Huang/NanoLab, colorized by Talbott/NIST; p. 35 Ria Novosti/Science Photo Library; p. 39 © P Cox/Alamy; p. 40 Bloomberg/Getty Images; p. 47 Suzanne Plunkett/ReutersLandov; p. 55 Don Bayley/iStock/Thinkstock; p. 59 Stephen Coburn/Shutterstock.com; p. 62 Visuals Unlimited, Inc./Victor Habbick/Getty Images; pp. 64–65 Ulrich Baumgarten/Getty Images; pp. 68–69 Raleigh News & Observer/McClatchy-Tribune/Getty Images; cover and interior pages design elements Zffoto/Shutterstock.com, Sergey Nivens/Shutterstock.com, elen_studio/Shutterstock.com, Lukas Rs/Shutterstock.com, Nucleartist/Shutterstock.com, Georg Preissl/Shutterstock.com, Jack1e/Shutterstock.com, Sfio Cracho/Shutterstock.com.

Designer: Michael Moy; Editor: Kathy Kuhtz Campbell